I Am Woman

I Am Woman

by
Yvonne M. Johnson

Accents Publishing • Lexington, Kentucky • 2022

Copyright © 2022 by Yvonne M. Johnson
All rights reserved

Printed in the United States of America

Accents Publishing
Editor: Katerina Stoykova-Klemer
Cover Image: *Girl in Garden* by Cassie Payne (*cassiepayneart.wixsite.com/casatlas*)

ISBN: 978-1-936628-87-2
First Edition

Accents Publishing is an independent press for brilliant voices. For a catalog of current and upcoming titles, please visit us on the Web at

www.accents-publishing.com

CONTENTS

The Performance / 1
The Vanishing / 2
Biologic / 3
Notice: My Body / 5
Clitoridectomy / 6
menarche. / 7
Rupture / 8
Hidden Spines / 9
Plastination / 10
Contraceptive / 11
Midwifery / 12
Vena Amoris / 13
Estrogen Quotient / 14
Rememory / 15
Haptic Memory / 16
Leukophobia / 17
The Red Scare / 18
Telegony / 19
Microchimerism / 21
The Bargain / 22
I am fear / 23
Intersexuality / 25
// Transcoded / 26
Because I love you / 28
The Husband Stitch / 29
Leiomyoma / 31
Thanatosis / 32
I dream / 33

Acknowledgments / 35

About the Author / 37

For all women

THE PERFORMANCE

They say the artist must be willing
to be naked, to rip flesh from her
own bones & give it to the world
for safekeeping. She must stand

before sleepless eyes & speak
our sins. She must ignore creeping
fingers & clattering teeth, hands
holding olive branches & knives

unsure which one they'll raise.
Because if she doesn't, if she
lets fear clench her tired muscles
close, she removes the voices

from the throats who need it most.
But she was never ready to be
a skeleton shivering on our stage.
She was never ready for the knives.

THE VANISHING

The doctor told my nana
her boy would absorb
his sister into his body

like sunlight. I like
to think he reminded
her of Unelanuhi's

daughter, who escaped
the ghost world as a red
bird. Let her imagine

her girl as a great hawk
or gentle finch just waiting
to unshackle herself.

Doctors cannot say
whether neurons firing
in dying fetal brains

comprehend vanishing.
Instead, it is left to the poet
to dissect magic tricks,

to explain how the girl
disappeared but left her
long beautiful spine in

her brother's back because
he needed hers, too,
to stand strong.

BIOLOGIC

we met in bed
on a hot evening
somewhere downtown

you pulled me against
your bloated belly
like we were old friends

or 2 ex-lovers bumping
into one another
but you had waited until

your body crumpled
to finally meet me
or learn my name

the small intestine is 7 meters
the tumor took $5/100^{th}$ of a meter
but it still impregnated you

like when 1 of 250 million
of your sperm made
my grandmother swell

& you split to make
6 other accidents
with different women

we met again in church
in front of a sweating pastor
who burst into song 4 times

he spoke of your sum
the 73 years of memories
you left for us to total

you were the color
of my momma
the $12.45 you left her

and the stench of you dying

NOTICE: MY BODY

My mom pouted when I rejected makeup
for prom or graduation. I let her brush
powder across my nose and plop rouge
on my lips. After, I no longer recognized
the unfreckled face in the vanity mirror.

My boyfriend didn't care if I shaved
less over winter, but the small hairs
between my eyebrows bothered him.
He told me he had tweezers I could
borrow. I plucked them the next week.

The boys on my track team laughed
after smelling *poontang* in the stretching
circle. They taught me about the smell
of my vagina—how it should be hidden
with frequent washes and scented soaps.

When classmates began asking if I was Indian
and their parents told them not to date me,
I learned that my mixed skin did not belong
in their colorless world. I still feel trapped
between two planets, unsure where to land.

Sometimes, my mom craned her neck
to study my cheeks. Her gaze always
lingered on the acne. I took a medicine
first used to treat cancer for clear skin.
I just wanted her to look me in the eyes.

CLITORIDECTOMY

for Nawal El Saadawi

I discovered my clit
at age eleven when
the spongy skin
of my inner thigh
rubbed against it
while turning
over in my sleep.

It was removed
that summer. I
wish I could say
it was men's
hands that held
me to the ground
and guided the blade.

Not my sister's, my
mother's, or the ones
belonging to the strange
woman who gripped
the razor like a butcher.
She threw dust on me
to stop the bleeding.

*Look—now you are pure,
now you are ready to marry.*
She frowned at my tears.
*Worry about bombs over your
head, guns in your streets.
Every day we are dying. How
do you weep over an orgasm?*

MENARCHE.[1]

    for Nikky Finney

the female clavicle is the sexiest bone period it connects
breast to body period it is reported to be illusive   hypnotic
period scientists say if a growing boy saw it he would forget
that $a^2 + b^2 = c^2$ or the kernel always runs in privileged mode.

the male nipple can lactate period its breast is appropriately small
period the female counterpart is strictly meant for intercourse period
in the case of indecent exposure females should apologize
profusely and promptly secure their cotton brassieres.

the female body is harmful to untrained eyes period its influence
requires more careful study period history shows it kills crops
and gives dogs rabies period judges state that approximately six inches
of epidermis have enough power to rip down the zipper of decent men.

a young female is expected to cover herself the first month she bleeds.

---

1 A woman's first menstruation.

RUPTURE

What's it like?
It's like the slimy
squish of new gum
right before it hardens
before sore jaws spit
out flavorless mound,
like fresh strip of tape
before it is covered
with hair or small bugs
before it is crumpled
on the way to trash can,
like the glide of white
shoes before they are too
black for comfort before
soles are rubbed raw,
like ripe fruit sitting
on countertop before
it rots before the stench
makes passersby gag.
It's like a young woman
losing her virginity.

HIDDEN SPINES

the female spent a lot of time
thinking about flies and felines.
sometimes she thought of them
after hearing the distant screech
of a queen yowling for a tom.

tomcats and chimpanzees
have barbs on their penises.
spines make quick work of sex
allowing for polyamorous
relationships and promiscuity.

the male had barbs once, too.
but they disappeared long
before he forced the female
to the ground and inserted his
favorite body part inside her.

the female knew this, of course.
but the way barbless skin raked
flesh raw always caused the female
to wonder if those tiny white
keratin spines ever actually left.

PLASTINATION[2]

The process begins with embalming. Formalin is pumped into the specimen's arteries to kill all bacteria and stop decay. Connective tissues are carefully removed.

I lost my skin 5 days after I died. They placed me between the woman who (embarrassingly) has her fetus showing and the couple really going at it (their stamina is miraculous).

An acetone bath effectively dissolves body fat. The specimen is placed into a vacuum chamber and is forcefully impregnated with silicon rubber. The polymer penetrates every cell.

I don't know what my vagina looks like, but this one anatomy teacher from Dayton sure does. And about 20 children. Pee doesn't come from the vagina, kids. (Was I supposed to know that?)

Now, the specimen is correctly positioned. In most cases, the specimen is ready after 8 to 12 months, but more complicated arrangements have been known to take up to 3 years.

After a year, my body was ready. I donated it, but I don't remember why. I just have to keep laughing, so I don't realize I'm in a museum of Hottentot Venuses.

---

[2] The technique used to preserve human specimens for Body Worlds exhibits.

CONTRACEPTIVE

> *Based on interviews from the
> Out-Migration Project: Urban
> Appalachian Women in Cincinnati,
> Ohio Oral History Project*

momma and daddy prayed
their silence about my body
would keep me innocent.

maybe i would've been
had my grade school
friend not taught me
about the place between
her legs that a whole
finger could slip through
or if that boy never tried
to convince me his parts
were different from mine.

when my teacher taught
me about abstinence
without explaining sex,
she and my parents agreed
that the older man i grew up
with and married at thirteen
was the best possible person
to introduce me to my body
and the son it would hold.

MIDWIFERY

> Based on an interview with Martha Lady,
> Frontier Nursing Service Oral History Project

I see it all the time
with the young girls—
the way they flinch
or widen their eyes
as the doctor presses
his gloved hand
into their abdomens

but it is always worse
when he asks them
to spread their legs
and he turns to pick
up the speculum he
will insert inside them

It is at this moment
when they are about
to cry or run or fight
I remember their faces
when we first walked in
how stoic they were

like they could handle
being naked and touched
and pregnant and alone
all at the same time
because they are woman
they are unbreakable
but they always shatter

VENA AMORIS[3]

> *Fathers and mothers are parting today*
> *There's dust on the altar where we used to pray*
>
> —Dust on the Altar sung by Jennifer O. Henderson,
> Out-Migration Project: Urban Appalachian Women
> in Cincinnati, Ohio Oral History Project

i never thought much about fingers
growing up unless i was digging
out the dirt underneath my nails
or sucking the blood away from

paper cuts. but the year after high
school, all my friends were showing
off their ring fingers and fiancés
like that was the next logical step.

we didn't marry for love. he said
it was all right that i didn't feel
that way. i wanted security, so
i gave him my finger and name.

marriage has a habit of turning
people into monsters. back home,
every story was the same. he abused
me. he wasn't faithful. he left me.

i've lived with my current partner
for years, but i'm never going to
marry him. i think a ring finger
is best without the collar.

---

[3] The "vein of love" that is thought to connect the ring finger of the left hand directly to the heart.

ESTROGEN QUOTIENT

> *To the daughters of Lawrence H. Summers,
> president of Harvard University (2001-2006)*

Were you surprised to learn
what your father believed
or did he draft his presentation
with you on his bouncing knee?

Perhaps he carefully spelled
out the intricacies of the female
brain after you failed
your first big exam:

because you are female
your brain is 10% smaller
has 6.5 times less gray matter
than the average man's

because you are woman
you have language centers
in both hemispheres predisposing
you to prefer words over numbers

because you are girl
your neural network
raises you to mother
and nurse and teach

Did he tell you that you'd
never be as smart as Tesla
or Turing because females
aren't born to be geniuses?

I can only hope you set
out to prove him wrong.

REMEMORY

She calls her vagina   a Rorschach blot
a crying baby   red and angry

lusting for any   lies disguised as
nipple teasing   puffy puckered lips

thirsty parts   refusing to open   wide
stay silent nine years   there never was a choice

        want to play a game?
           let's
              find

the clit

touched too early   fingerprint stains on fresh paper
by a horny man   in *all* the wrong places

she never liked   blood or ketchup
the poor thing   be murder or foreplay

it reminds her of   a splatter on parchment
a stillborn fetus   is nothing more than ink

HAPTIC MEMORY

I saw his shaking hands
when you touched me there
I had not thought about him
for years & in a moment
you were him   the woods
and his undone zipper

Maybe you had a right
to know why I folded
myself like a fetus
why any body wants
to remember being
inside a mother's womb

why I still have to check
if the arm around my torso
the breath across my neck
or the legs between my thighs
really belong to the man
I allowed to touch me

LEUKOPHOBIA[4]

She is afraid of teeth
above her pubic hair
& fingernails tracing

her waistline Of large
pimples & wet underwear
She is afraid of semen

So, touch her like a newborn
covered in birth   like papaw's
slim honeycomb bones

She has scar tissue
calluses on heels
& deodorant stains

the sleep left in eyes
dead skin & saliva
She has silver curls

Do not bruise her skin
drug her hemophilic blood
or claim her sweat

Do not be so eager
to enter her womb

---

[4] The fear of the color white.

THE RED SCARE

I could have been pregnant
but never gave any urine
or blood to know for sure

Each day I woke with clean
underwear anxiety curled
around my heart like a feline
at a sleeper's unguarded neck
my pulse skipping nine beats

I never once imagined
my stomach growing
to the size of a watermelon
or tiny brown limbs pushing
against my stretching skin

I was on the exam table
with my feet in stirrups
& metal tongs reaching
into my womb to remove
that gross unwanted *thing*

I refused to envy them
grandmother mother sister
young committed women
too brave   too foolish
to kill for convenience

I cried when my period came
It was heavy & vibrant
like an early miscarriage

TELEGONY[5]

> *My skin is tan*
> *My hair is fine*
> *My hips invite you*
> *My mouth like wine*
>
> —Nina Simone

i taught you to pretend
you like the caress of tongue
against cheek against teeth

to not smell puke or piss
or feel him inside of you
but sound like you do

i taught you to charge extra
when he doesn't pull out
to like the names he calls you

i will not teach you to watch
a fruit fly lay her eggs
inside of rotten tomatoes

to wait for them to hatch
and notice they have
the same bulging thorax

of her first partner
the wings of her third
and the daddy's wide eyes

i do not want you to know
that he will linger inside of you
longer than his dead sperm

---

[5] The scientific theory that a child can inherit characteristics from all of the female's sexual partners and not just the father. This phenomenon is observed in fruit flies.

that your baby will have
his long bony hands
or his square nose

that your son will look
like every damn man
who crosses your threshold

MICROCHIMERISM[6]

the first son was torn
limb by limb from womb

the second you didn't know
you miscarried his first week

the third was born still
—he fit in your dry palm

each son left y chromosomes
in your bloodstream

when your daughter was born
you passed these cells to her

somehow after all these years
the dead refuse to leave

---

6   The presence of male Y chromosomes in a mother's body.

THE BARGAIN

It's always been this moment
the slow part of lips
the convergence of two heads
the desiring of new woman

It's always been this moment
when I determine the price
of my own skin and who
is allowed to pay the toll

It's always been this moment
just before he throws a soft wad
of bills and three silver coins
next to my unsatisfied body

still knelt over like a bitch
or a forgotten goddess
It's always been this power
why I search for it again

and again and again

I AM FEAR

It is 3am when I wake
to the stranger climbing
up the ladder to my bed.
It is 3am when I feel
his hand brush my ankle.

I cannot curse like
I want to. I cannot
move like I want to.
Instead, I am weak.
I am soundless sobs.

& he is breath. When
it is over, he is silence.
I can hear the slumbering
lungs of all the men
in my hostel room.

I cannot call for help like
I want to. I cannot trust
these men like I want to.
So my limbs carry me
past shadowed bodies.

There is a man at reception.
Was he drunk is his first
question like a drunk man
should be excused or could be
forgiven. *I don't want to cause*

a scene he says. I do not argue.
I am pathetic. Instead, I let
him lead me to a private room

& I leave the stranger sleeping
because he is man & I am woman.

& I am already so much loss.

INTERSEXUALITY

there is space below covers
the length of naked bodies
phantom limbs set together
against waists after pouring
hard & sturdy like concrete

a quiet word a fake orgasm
in a deep voice hides raw flesh
vibrates chests delays periods
for decades beckons doctors'
buries itself with hands to feel
the lump beneath a stomach's pit

a fear of scalpels separating skin
or ripping organs from person
reminds the brain like sandpaper
    how the curious finger
the surgical knife cold quick & sure
cut off their penis widened their vagina

// TRANSCODED

```cpp
#include "Person.h"

using namespace HomeSweetHome;

string remember() {
        Person eli, momma, daddy, boys;
        eli.setGender("boy");
        eli.setAge(8);
        eli.setGender("girl?");
        eli.setAge(13);
        eli.setGender("unknown");
        try {
                while(!finished) {
                    eli.use("momma's high heels");
                    eli.use("lipstick");
                    if(footsteps == true) {
                        throw momma_is_coming;
                    }
                    footsteps = true;
                }
        } catch (momma_is_coming) {
                eli.abandonTask();
                momma.smack(eli);
                momma.hug(eli);
                momma.cry();
        }
        eli.setAge(17);
        eli.setGender("woman");
        eli.setPronouns("her", "she");
        daddy.say("abomination");
        daddy.say("God ain't acceptin' no sissie-ass f~~aggots~~");
        momma.say("...");
```

```
        eli.wear("dress");
        eli.wear("makeup");
        eli.goTo("party");
        eli.drink();
        eli.drink();
        eli.drink();
        eli.feel("funny");
        boys.say("Hey, look at the trap.");
        boys.say("Do you think he still has a penis?");
        boys.surround(eli);
        boys.holdDown(eli);
        boys.touch(eli);
        boys.laugh();

        eli.feel("wrong");
        eli.lookIn("mirror");
        eli.washOff("mascara");
        eli.tryTo("breathe");

        return "me too";
}
```

BECAUSE I LOVE YOU

for Vanessa Guillen

I want you to stay silent
about the things he said

give him a small smile
chuckle at his crude jokes

I want you to be gentle
when you tell him no

pretend you have a boyfriend
remain innocent   sweet

Because I love you

I do not want you
to become a hashtag

to hear how he slammed
a hammer against your head

to see the face of the woman
who cut you into rough pieces

Because I need you to stay alive
Because I need you

Because

THE HUSBAND STITCH

for Carmen Maria Machado

She remembers the doctor
She remembers the mouth
remembers watching it
from the hospital bed
as it spoke about episiotomies,
the perineum, & the crowning
of her son's head. It asked her
permission to slide a scalpel

into her skin, a small incision
from her vulva to her anus,
but did not wait for her answer.
Maybe it did not matter what
the woman wanted, maybe
the body of her unborn son
was more important than
her own. The mouth told

her not to worry, that she
would be stitched up nice
& tight. She remembers
holding her son for the
first time. She remembers
scar tissue & the pain of sex,
remembers retreating to the web
to search for familiar whispers.

I was forced to have a c-section.
The husband stitch—it's real.
Maybe these women are exceptions,
anomalies of a working health system,

conspiracy theorists who misremember
& believe in the imaginary. Maybe it does
not matter how many women whisper
or shout, maybe no one is around to listen.

LEIOMYOMA[7]

inspired by an interview with KalaLea
Bodies Podcast—Episode 2: Bleeding

the mother was informed by police
after her children were already gone.
only the strange, foul fruit of her country
were left dangling from tree branches
or sprawled carelessly across blacktop,

split open next to the ring bearing
his father's name, skittles melting
in Florida heat, a toy gun underneath
the swing set, six damn bullet casings
on asphalt. did you see them there?

& when she had no more Black
children for her countrymen to take
with frayed nooses or bloody fists,
they took her uterus, grew fibroids
in her womb the size of grapefruits.

every month brought heavy, painful
periods like a red record stuck on repeat
until hands pulled womb from tired body.
hungry fingers threatened by unarmed
Black bodies harvested her motherhood,

& all you told her was *all lives matter.*

---

[7] Usually benign tumors that grow in the uterus, also known as fibroids. As Black women are more affected by fibroids than white women, researchers theorize that these tumors are one of the physical effects of racism on the female body.

THANATOSIS[8]

I dreamt of being an entomologist
as a child, of studying beetles
underneath my magnifying glass

& raising massive ant colonies
inside transparent boxes. Even now
I dream of dragonflies, watch female

Moorland Hawkers crashing to the Earth,
feigning death to escape horny pursuers.
I want it to be that easy. To be left alone

when I sleep. To be safe when I am
unconscious. But men are not dragonflies
& I cannot hide inside tall grass.

---

8   The act of playing dead to avoid unwanted sexual attention—often seen in insects.

I DREAM

of being raped while walking
home at night. Sometimes
there are people passing
pretending they cannot see

or hear me. & when I wake
I read about the obscenity
of my breasts, about the mother
charged as a sex offender

for being topless in her own home.
I hear debates about the personhood
of my womb, how birth control
is abortion & I am powerless.

I am afraid to get drunk
to walk alone & have sex.
I am afraid to be a woman
to have to explain to a judge

what I did to make him do it
& then watch him become
a supreme court justice, receive
one year of house arrest or walk free.

I am no longer sure
when I am dreaming.

ACKNOWLEDGMENTS

This book would not exist without the love, time, patience, wisdom, and encouragement of several people dear to my heart.

Thank you to Katerina and everyone at Accents Publishing because without you these poems would be nothing more than bits on my hard drive.

To my Kentucky Governor's School for the Arts instructors and the Affrilachian Poets, many thanks for introducing me to my inner poet and for the critiques that saved everyone from having to read the first drafts of these poems.

Cassie, thank you for the stunning cover. I cannot imagine a better artwork to complement this work.

Finally, thank you to my parents who never once tried to discourage the little girl announcing that she was going to grow up and be an author—because of you, I always felt like my dreams were possible.

ABOUT THE AUTHOR

Yvonne M. Johnson graduated from the University of Kentucky with degrees in English and Computer Science. As an undergraduate, she was inducted as an Affrilachian Poet, served as president of her university's creative writing club, and was managing poetry and German language editor of the undergraduate literary journal. She also holds a master's degree in cyber security from Lancaster University in England, which she completed on a Fulbright scholarship. When she is not writing, she can be found riding horses, training her Labrador to find missing people, and legally hacking into her customers' computer systems.